Your first 100 words in GERMAN

German for Total Beginners Through Puzzles and Games

Series concept
Jane Wightwick

Illustrations
Mahmoud Gaafar

German edition
Teresa Braunwalder

McGraw-Hill

Chicago New York San Francisco Lisbon London Madrid Mexico City
Milan New Delhi San Juan Seoul Singapore Sydney Toronto

McGraw-Hill

A Division of The McGraw-Hill Companies

1 2 3 4 5 6 7 8 9 0   VLP/VLP   1 0 9 8 7 6 5 4 3 2

ISBN 0-07-139600-4

Printed and bound by Vicks Lithograph

Cover design by Nick Panos

McGraw-Hill books are available at special quantity discounts to use as premiums and sales promotions, or for use in corporate training programs. For more information, please write to the Director of Special Sales, Professional Publishing, McGraw-Hill, Two Penn Plaza, New York, NY 10121-2298. Or contact your local bookstore.

This book is printed on acid-free paper.

◎ CONTENTS

Flashcards (8 sheets of tear-out topic flashcards)

⊚ HOW TO USE THIS BOOK

In this activity book you'll find 100 key German words and phrases. All of the activities are designed specifically for developing confidence in the early stages of learning a language. Many of the activities are inspired by the kind of games used to teach children to read their own language: flashcards, matching games, memory games, joining exercises, anagrams, etc. This is not only a more effective method of learning new words, but also much more fun.

We've included an **Introduction** to get you started. This is a friendly introduction to German pronunciation and spelling that will give you tips on how to say and memorize the words.

Then you can move on to the 8 **Topics**. Each topic presents essential words with pictures to help memorization. There is a pronunciation guide so you know how to say each word. These words are also featured in the tear-out **Flashcard** section at the back of the book. When you've mastered the words, you can go on to try the activities and games for that topic.

Finally, there's a **Round-up** section to review all your new words and the **Answers** to all the activities to check yourself.

Follow this 4-step plan for maximum success:

1 Have a look at the key topic words with their pictures. Then tear out the flashcards and shuffle them. Put them German side up. Try to say the word and remember what it means. Then turn the card over to check with the English.

2 Put the cards English side up and try to say the German word. Try the cards again each day both ways around. (When you can remember a card for 7 days in a row, you can file it!)

3 Try out the activities and games for each topic. This will reinforce your recognition of the key words.

4 After you have covered all the topics, you can try the activities in the Round-up section to test your knowledge of all the German words in the book. You can also try shuffling all the 100 flashcards together to see how many you can remember.

This flexible and fun way of learning your first words in German should give you a head start whether you're studying at home or in a group.

◎ INTRODUCTION

The purpose of this section is to introduce the basic principles of how German is written and pronounced. If you understand these principles, you will have a head start when it comes to learning your first words. Concentrate on the main points. The details will come as you progress.

Have a quick look at this section and try to produce the sounds out loud, in a confident manner and then move on to the topics for some practice. As you work your way through the words in this activity book, you will find the spelling and pronunciation gradually start to come more naturally.

◎ A logical language

German is a logical language. Concepts are often expressed by combining short words where English would use a separate item of vocabulary. For example:

Schrank	cupboard
Kühlschrank	refrigerator, literally "cool cupboard"
Last	weight/load
Lastwagen	truck, literally "load cart"

This aspect of the language, and the many similar words in English and German (see page 8), can help you increase your vocabulary and work out new words.

◎ Pronunciation tips

Many German letters are pronounced in a similar way to their English equivalents, but here are some differences to watch out for. It is these differences that trip up the beginner so try to look over this list and say the words out loud using the pronunciation guide (underscoring indicates the stress: see page 6). Be aware that the suggested pronunciations are approximate and don't take in regional variations; and there will always be some exceptions to the rules.

j	like *y* in "yet," e.g. **ja** *yah* (yes)
w	like *v* in "vase," e.g. **Wald** *vald* (forest)
v	like *f* as in "feet," e.g. **wie viel?** *vee feel* (how much?)
z/tz	like *ts* in "its," e.g. **jetzt** *yetst* (now)
r	a German **r** is rolled at the back of the throat, e.g. **Regen** *raigen* (rain)
ch	a German **ch** can be pronounced "hard" like the Yiddish "*ch*utzpah," written as *kh* in the pronunciation guide, e.g. **Bauch** *bowkh* (stomach); or "softly" like *y* in "you," written as *gh* in the pronunciation guide, e.g. **Teppich** *tepigh* (rug)

s	a German **s** can be pronounced *s*, e.g. **das** *das* (the); or (before a vowel) pronounced *z*, e.g. **Hose** <u>*hoh*</u>*zer* (pants). Before a **t** or **p** it sounds more like *sh*, e.g. **Stuhl** *shtool* (chair)
sch	like *sh* as in "*sh*eet," e.g. **Schule** <u>*shoo*</u>*ler* (school)
ß	a double *ss*, always used after a long vowel, e.g. **Straße** <u>*shtrah*</u>*sser* (street)

German vowels can be pronounced long or short:

e	can be pronounced *e* like "b*e*t," e.g. **Feld** *feld* (field); or *ai* like " f*air*," e.g. **der** *dair* (the). At the end of a word an **e** is pronounced close to the English *uh*, e.g. **Hose** <u>*ho*</u>*zuh* (pants).
a	can be pronounced *a* like "b*a*t," e.g. **Affe** <u>*aff*</u>*uh* (monkey); or *ah* like "b*ah*," e.g. **Schaf** *shahf* (sheep)
o	can be pronounced *o* like "g*o*t," e.g. **Rock** *rok* (skirt); or *oh* like "*Oh!*," e.g. **Hose** <u>*hoh*</u>*zer* (pants)
u	can be pronounced *u* like "b*u*t," e.g. **Hund** *hunnd* (dog); or *oo* like "z*oo*," e.g. **Hut** *hoot* (hat)

Watch out in particular for these combinations. Some of them are tricky as they look like familiar English sounds, but are pronounced differently in German:

au	like *ow* as in "n*ow*," e.g. **Haus** *hows* (house)
eu	like *oy* in "t*oy*," e.g. **neu** *noy* (new)
ee	like *ay* in "pl*ay*," e.g. **See** *zay* (lake)
ie	like *ee* in "f*ee*t," e.g. **die** *dee* (the). Don't confuse with **ei** below.
ei	like *i* in "f*i*ne" or *ie* in "t*ie*," e.g. **Bein** *bine* (leg)

✔ German often uses combinations of shorter words to express concepts

✔ Many German letters are pronounced the same as English, but some need special attention

✔ **e** at the end of a word is always pronounced, e.g. **Hose** = <u>*hoh*</u>*zuh*; **Blume** = <u>*bloo*</u>*muh*

◎ Umlaut

An Umlaut is two dots written above a letter (¨). It can be written on one of three vowels and changes their pronunciation:

- **ü**, pronounced *ew* as in **Hügel** *hewgel* (hill)

- **ä**, pronounced *e* as in **Bäcker** *beker* (baker)

- **ö**, pronounced *ur* as in **schön** *shurn* (beautiful)

◎ Capital letters

German nouns (naming words) are *always* written with an initial capital letter, whether or not they begin a sentence, e.g. **die Schule** (the school). *It is very important to remember these capital letters when you are writing German.*

◎ Stress

In English, the first syllable of a word is usually emphasized or said slightly louder than the rest of the word (<u>fac</u>tory, <u>win</u>dow, <u>rab</u>bit). German also usually stresses the first syllable but there are a few exceptions, e.g. **Fabrik** *fa<u>brik</u>* (factory), **Kaninchen** *ka<u>nee</u>nghen* (rabbit). The stress is shown in this book by underscoring.

- ✔ The German accent is called **Umlaut** (ü, ä, ö) and affects pronunciation
- ✔ All German nouns are written with a capital letter
- ✔ German word stress varies

◎ Masculine, feminine, and neuter

In English, the definite article is always "the," e.g. "the table," "the door," "the window." In German, nouns are either masculine (<u>der</u> Tisch), feminine (<u>die</u> Tür) or neuter (<u>das</u> Fenster) and the word for "the" varies accordingly. In the plural it is usually **die** as in **die Haare** (literally "the hairs").

It is important as you progress in German to know whether a word is masculine, feminine or neuter and, for this reason, we have given the 100 words with their articles. Try to get used to learning new words this way – it will help you later.

Similar words

German has many words which sound and mean the same as English but are spelled differently. Sound them out using the guidelines in this introduction and you will recognize them, e.g. **Schuh, Fisch, Maus, Haus.**

Here are some more examples of words that are very similar in German and English. With these words and the 100 key words in this book, you will already have made progress more quickly than you imagined possible.

das Taxi, pronounced as the English   **der Bus**, pronounced *buss*

das Hotel, pronounced as the English   **das Telefon**, pronounced as the English

das Restaurant, pronounced *restohroñ*   **der Elefant**, pronounced *aile<u>fant</u>*

die Shorts, pronounced as the English   **das Museum**, pronounced *moo<u>zay</u>um*

✔   German nouns are either masculine (**der**), feminine (**die**), or neuter (**das**)

✔   There are many similar words in English and German

German alphabet

Here is the complete German alphabet with the names of the letters. These can be useful if you need to spell something – your own name for example.

A	*ah*	J	*yot*	S	*ess*
Ä	*eh*	K	*kah*	ß	*ess tset*
B	*bay*	L	*el*	T	*tay*
C	*tsay*	M	*em*	U	*oo*
D	*day*	N	*en*	Ü	*ew*
E	*ay*	O	*oh*	V	*fow*
F	*ef*	Ö	*ur*	W	*vay*
G	*gay*	P	*pay*	X	*ix*
H	*hah*	Q	*koo*	Y	*<u>ewp</u>sillon*
I	*ee*	R	*err*	Z	*tset*

AROUND THE HOME

Look at the pictures of things you might find in a house.
Tear out the flashcards for this topic.
Follow steps 1 and 2 of the plan in the introduction.

das Fenster
das fenster

der Stuhl
dair shtool

der Tisch
dair tish

der Teppich
dair tepigh

der Computer
dair compyooter

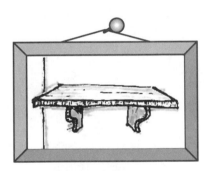

das Bord
das bord

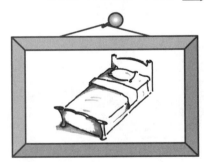

das Sofa   *das zofa*

das Bett   *das bett*

der Kühlschrank
dair kewlshrank

der Schrank
dair shrank

der Herd
dair haird

die Tür
dee tewr

Match the pictures with the words, as in the example.

das Sofa

das Bett

das Fenster

der Tisch

der Teppich

der Computer

das Bord

der Stuhl

Now match the German household words to the English.

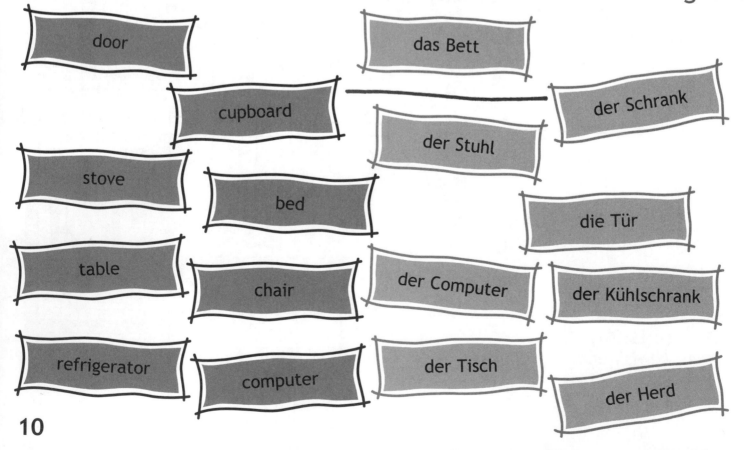

door

das Bett

cupboard

der Schrank

der Stuhl

stove

bed

die Tür

table

chair

der Computer

der Kühlschrank

refrigerator

computer

der Tisch

der Herd

◎ **F**ill in the missing letters in these household words.

S _ u h _   S c _ _ a _ _

_ o r _   F _ _ s _ _ r

T _ p _ _ c _   _ ü _

_ ü h _ s _ h r _ n _   B _ _ t

_ e r _   _ i s _ _

- -

◎ **S**ee if you can find these objects in the word square.
The words can run left to right, or top to bottom:

H	E	R	D	P	I	S	D
S	G	S	T	U	H	L	P
O	H	L	D	R	B	A	T
F	E	N	S	T	E	R	I
A	L	A	O	E	T	A	S
I	R	C	F	A	T	S	C
G	T	E	P	P	I	C	H
O	E	P	O	R	T	A	T

11

Decide where the household items should go. Then write the correct number in the picture, as in the example.

1 der Tisch 2 der Stuhl 3 das Sofa 4 der Teppich

5 das Bord 6 das Bett 7 der Schrank 8 der Herd

9 der Kühlschrank 10 der Computer 11 das Fenster 12 die Tür

Choose the German word that matches the picture and fill in the English word at the bottom of the page.

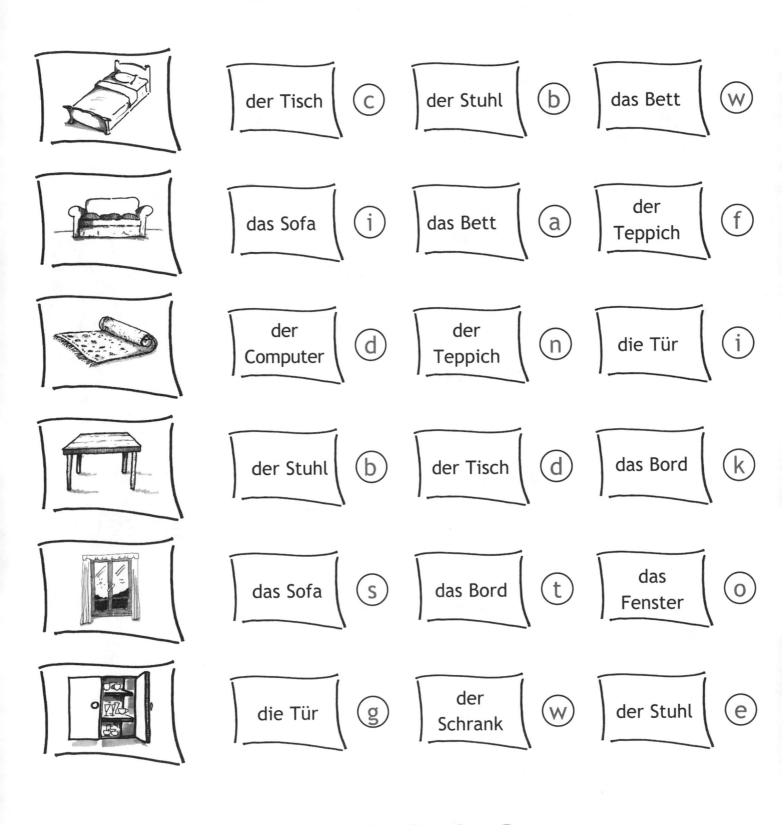

der Tisch — c   der Stuhl — b   das Bett — w

das Sofa — i   das Bett — a   der Teppich — f

der Computer — d   der Teppich — n   die Tür — i

der Stuhl — b   der Tisch — d   das Bord — k

das Sofa — s   das Bord — t   das Fenster — o

die Tür — g   der Schrank — w   der Stuhl — e

English word: w ◯ ◯ ◯ ◯ ◯

2 CLOTHES

Look at the pictures of different clothes.
Tear out the flashcards for this topic.
Follow steps 1 and 2 of the plan in the introduction.

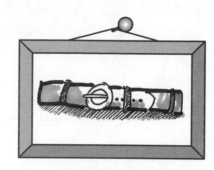

der Gürtel
dair gewrtel

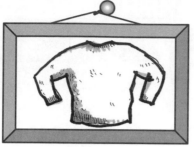

der Pullover
dair pullohver

die Socke
dee zokuh

der Schlips
dair shlips

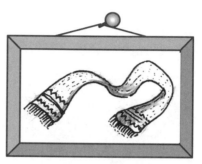

der Schal
dair shahl

die Hose
dee hohzuh

das Kleid
das klide

der Schuh
dair shoo

der Mantel
dair manntel

der Rock
dair rok

der Hut
dair hoot

das Hemd *das hemd*

14

Unscramble the letters to spell items of clothing.

Write the words with **der**, **die**, or **das**, remembering the intitial capital letter.

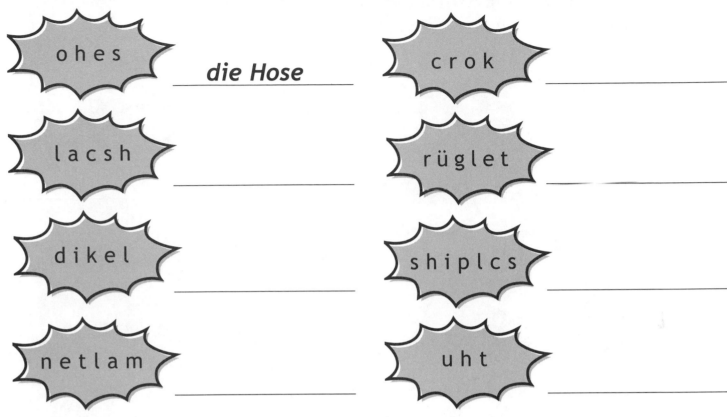

o h e s   *die Hose*   c r o k

l a c s h   r ü g l e t

d i k e l   s h i p l c s

n e t l a m   u h t

- -

See if you can find these clothes in the word square.

The words can run left to right, or top to bottom:

F	A	P	C	R	O	C	K
I	M	U	H	S	R	A	L
C	A	L	S	O	C	K	E
J	N	L	M	E	B	L	I
A	T	A	H	O	S	E	D
P	E	G	E	I	S	N	A
C	L	O	M	S	U	D	E
H	E	R	D	E	N	N	T

15

◎ **N**ow match the German words, their pronunciation, and the English meaning, as in the example.

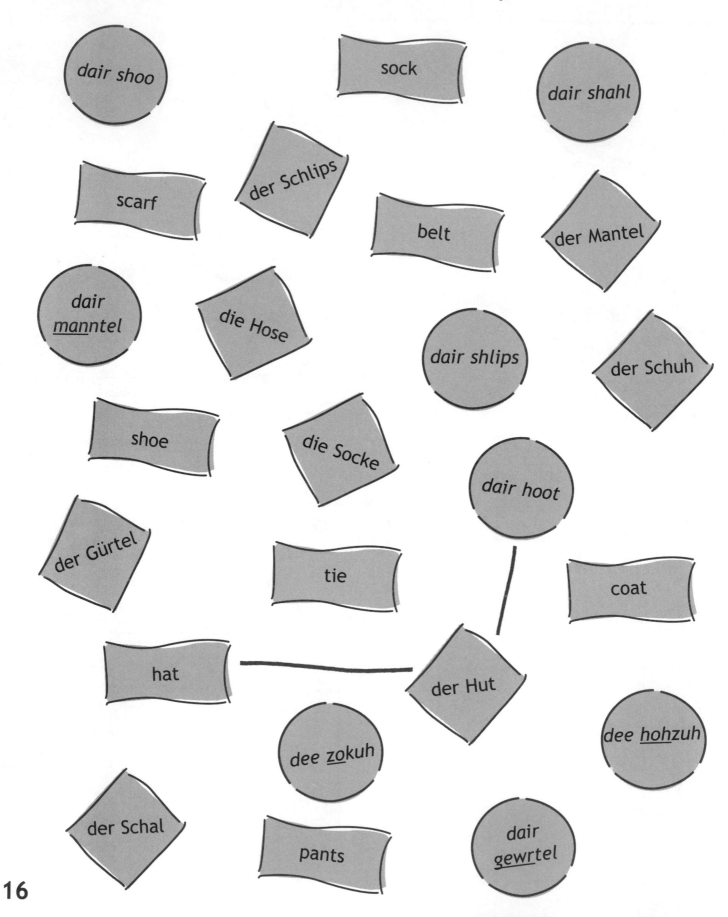

dair shoo

sock

dair shahl

scarf

der Schlips

belt

der Mantel

dair _manntel_

die Hose

dair shlips

der Schuh

shoe

die Socke

dair hoot

der Gürtel

tie

coat

hat

der Hut

dee _zokuh_

dee _hohzuh_

der Schal

pants

dair _gewrtel_

Carl is going on vacation. Count how many of each type of clothing he is packing in his suitcase.

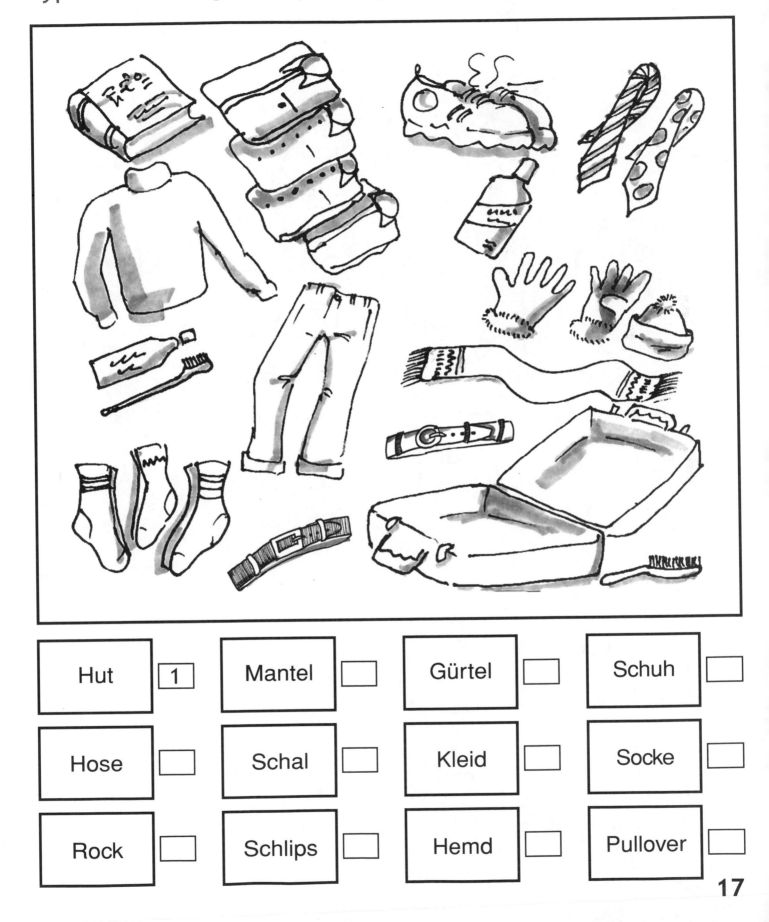

Hut — 1	Mantel —	Gürtel —	Schuh —
Hose —	Schal —	Kleid —	Socke —
Rock —	Schlips —	Hemd —	Pullover —

Someone has ripped up the German words for clothes. Can you join the two halves of the words, as the example?

Ro

Kle

Hu

He

Mant

Ho

uh

Schli

Sch

Gür

ke

se

ck

tel

el

id

t

Soc

md

ps

18

③ AROUND TOWN

Look at the pictures of things you might find around town.
Tear out the flashcards for this topic.
Follow steps 1 and 2 of the plan in the introduction.

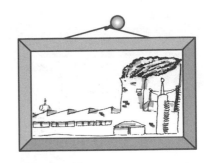

die Fabrik *dee fabrik*

der Bäcker
dair beker

das Haus
das howss

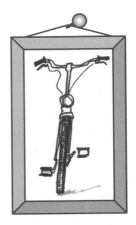

das Fahrrad
das fahr-rahd

das Auto
das owto

der Lastwagen
dair lastvagen

der Brunnen
dair brunnen

die Bank *dee bank*

die Schule *dee shooluh*

die Straße
dee shtrahssuh

der Laden *dair lahden*

der Metzger
dair metsger

Match the German words to their English equivalents.

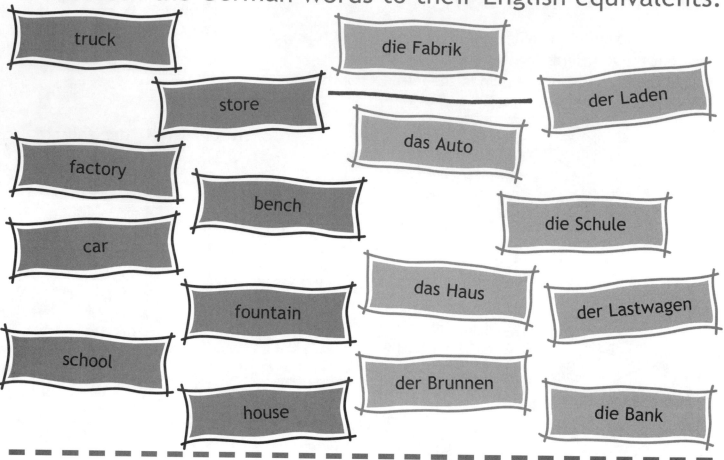

truck

die Fabrik

store

der Laden

das Auto

factory

bench

die Schule

car

das Haus

der Lastwagen

fountain

school

der Brunnen

house

die Bank

Now put the English words in the same order as the German word chain, as in the example.

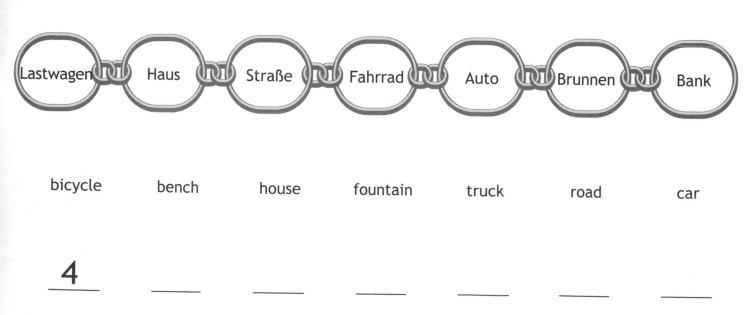

Lastwagen — Haus — Straße — Fahrrad — Auto — Brunnen — Bank

bicycle   bench   house   fountain   truck   road   car

<u>4</u>   ___   ___   ___   ___   ___   ___

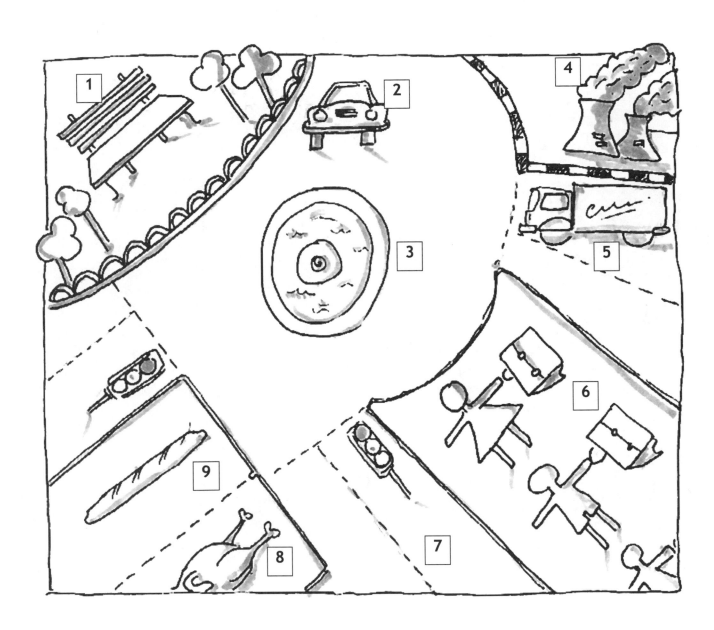

Label this town plan, as in the example.

1 *die Bank*   **2** _____   **3** _____

4 _____   **5** _____   **6** _____

7 _____   **8** _____   **9** _____

21

○ **C**hoose the German word that matches the picture and fill in the English word at the bottom of the page.

	die Bank (c)	das Auto (b)	das Haus (s)
	die Straße (c)	die Schule (a)	der Bäcker (f)
	der Brunnen (h)	das Auto (n)	der Metzger (i)
	das Haus (b)	das Fahrrad (o)	der Brunnen (k)
	die Schule (o)	die Straße (t)	die Fabrik (s)
	die Fabrik (g)	der Laden (w)	der Lastwagen (l)

English word: (s) ( ) ( ) ( ) ( ) ( )

⊚ **W**rite the words in the correct column, as in the example.

der	die	das
der Laden		

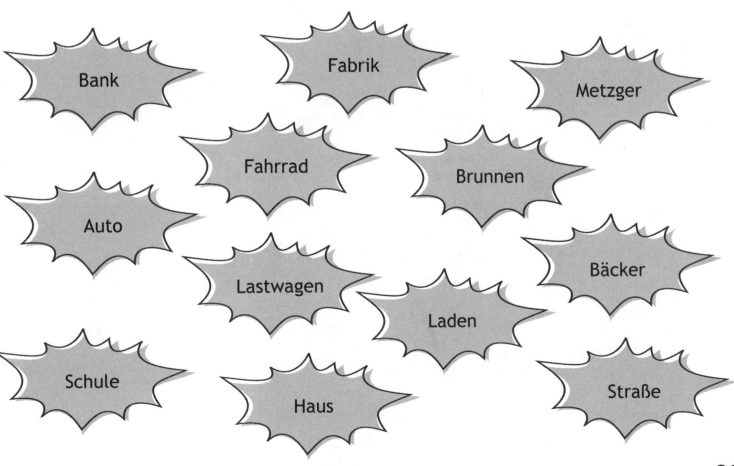

Bank

Fabrik

Metzger

Fahrrad

Brunnen

Auto

Bäcker

Lastwagen

Laden

Schule

Straße

Haus

④ COUNTRYSIDE

Look at the pictures of features you might find in the countryside.
Tear out the flashcards for this topic.
Follow steps 1 and 2 of the plan in the introduction.

der Hügel
dair hewgel

die Brücke
dee brewkuh

der Bauernhof
dair bowern-hohf

der Berg
dair bairg

der See
dair zay

der Baum
dair bowm

die Blume
dee bloomuh

der Fluss *dair fluss*

das Meer *das mair*

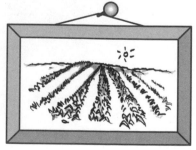

das Feld *das feld*

der Regen
dair raigen

der Wald
dair vald

Can you match all the countryside words to the pictures.

der Berg

der Bauernhof

das Meer

der Wald

der Regen

der Hügel

der See

die Brücke

der Fluss

die Blume

der Baum

das Feld

◎ **N**ow check (✔) the features you can find in this landscape.

Brücke	✔	Baum	☐	Regen	☐	Hügel	☐
Berg	☐	Meer	☐	Feld	☐	Wald	☐
See	☐	Fluss	☐	Blume	☐	Bauernhof	☐

◎ Unscramble the letters to reveal natural features.

Write the words with **der**, **die**, or **das**.

n e r g e *der Regen* _____

c e b ü r k _____

s l u f s _____

b o u f a h e r n _____

m a b u _____

e e s _____

e r m e _____

l e g ü h _____

- -

◎ See if you can find 8 countryside words in the square.

The words can run left to right, or top to bottom:

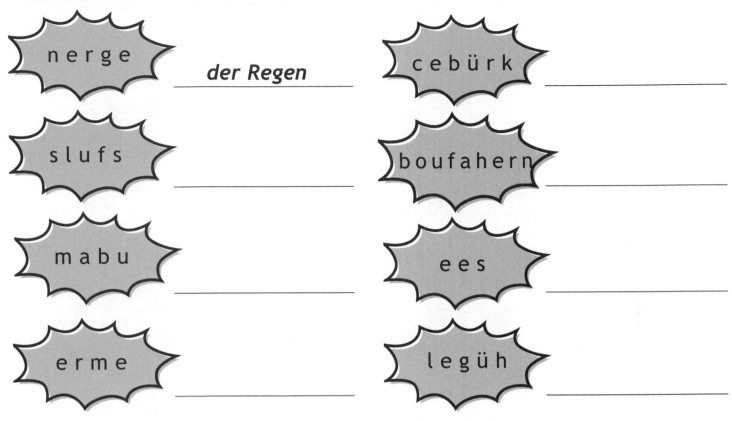

T	E	P	C	D	A	P	E
I	C	C	F	L	U	S	S
F	L	R	E	G	E	N	F
C	B	B	L	E	R	T	L
W	A	L	D	M	E	R	B
A	U	U	N	I	S	E	E
U	M	M	T	A	G	N	R
P	E	E	A	E	N	N	G

© **F**inally, test yourself by joining the German words, their pronunciation, and the English meanings, as in the example.

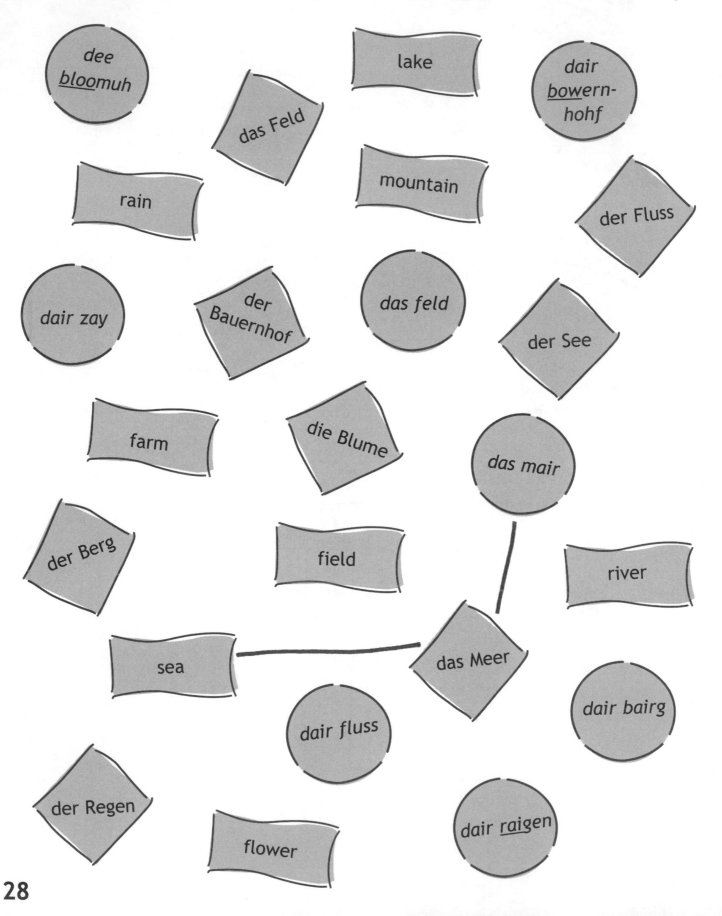

dee _bloomuh_

lake

dair _bowern-hohf_

das Feld

mountain

der Fluss

rain

dair zay

der Bauernhof

das feld

der See

farm

die Blume

das mair

der Berg

field

river

sea

das Meer

dair bairg

dair fluss

der Regen

dair _raigen_

flower

⑤ OPPOSITES

Look at the pictures.
Tear out the flashcards for this topic.
Follow steps 1 and 2 of the plan in the introduction.

schmutzig
shmutsigh

sauber
zowber

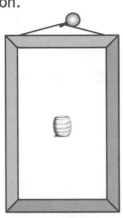

klein
kline

groß
grohss

billig *billigh*

leicht *lieght*

langsam *langzam*

teuer *toyer*

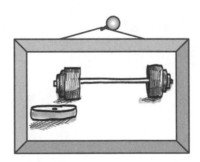

schwer *shvair*

schnell *shnell*

alt *alt*

neu *noy*

Join the German words to their English equivalents.

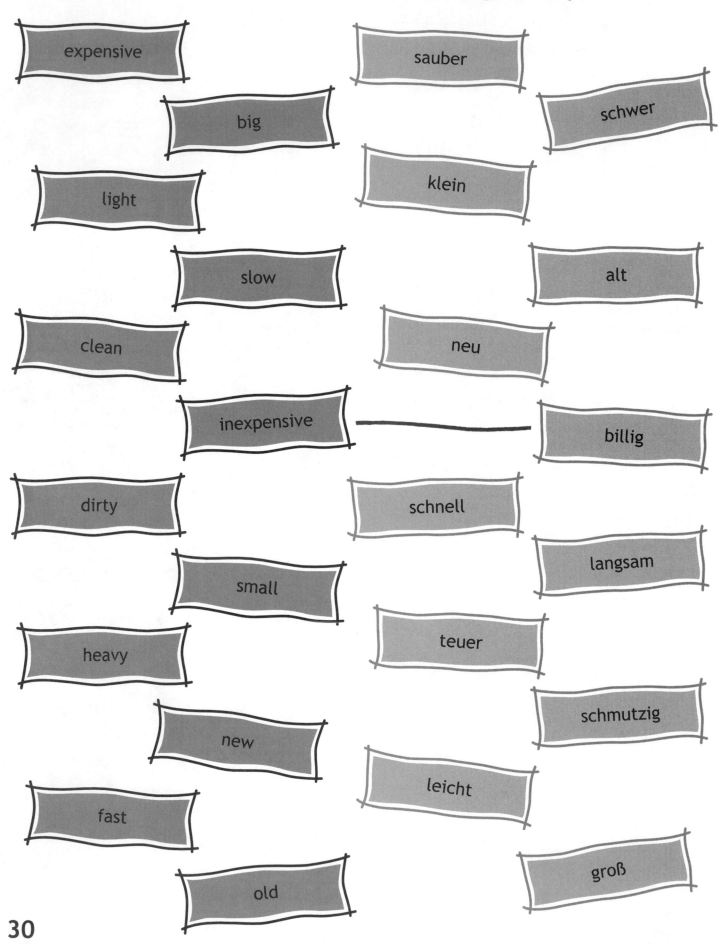

expensive

sauber

big

schwer

klein

light

slow

alt

clean

neu

inexpensive ———— billig

dirty

schnell

small

langsam

heavy

teuer

new

schmutzig

fast

leicht

old

groß

© **N**ow choose the German word that matches the picture to fill in the English word at the bottom of the page.

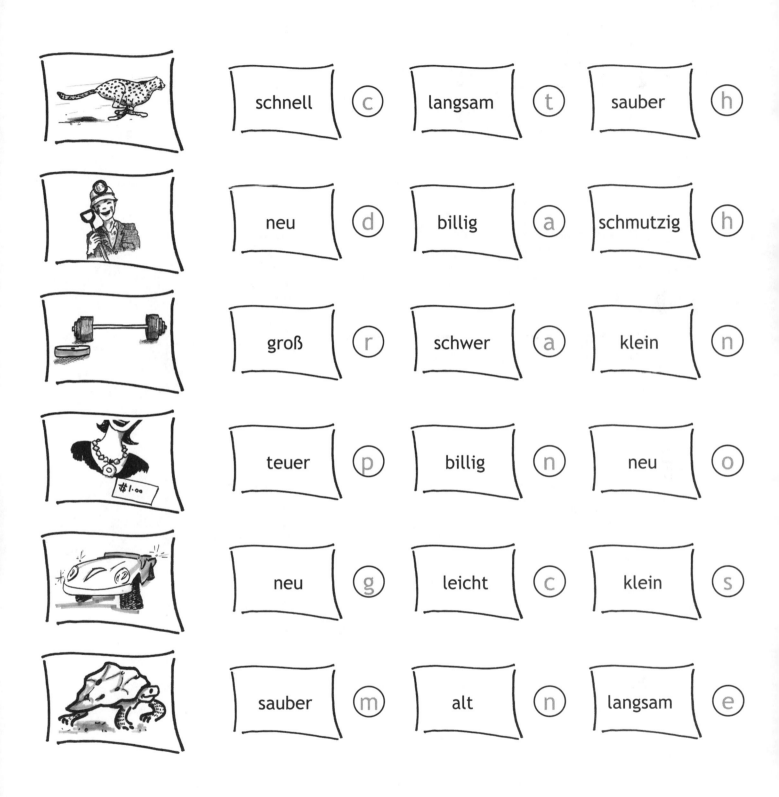

schnell Ⓒ	langsam Ⓣ	sauber Ⓗ
neu Ⓓ	billig Ⓐ	schmutzig Ⓗ
groß Ⓡ	schwer Ⓐ	klein Ⓝ
teuer Ⓟ	billig Ⓝ	neu Ⓞ
neu Ⓖ	leicht Ⓒ	klein Ⓢ
sauber Ⓜ	alt Ⓝ	langsam Ⓔ

English word: Ⓒ ◯ ◯ ◯ ◯ ◯

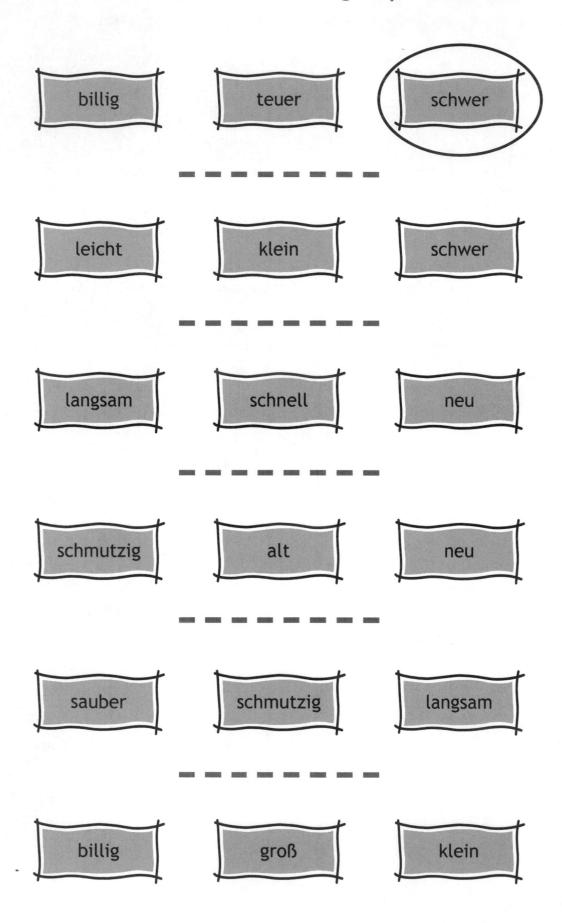

◎ **F**ind the odd one out in these groups of words.

billig   teuer   ⬭ schwer ⬭

leicht   klein   schwer

langsam   schnell   neu

schmutzig   alt   neu

sauber   schmutzig   langsam

billig   groß   klein

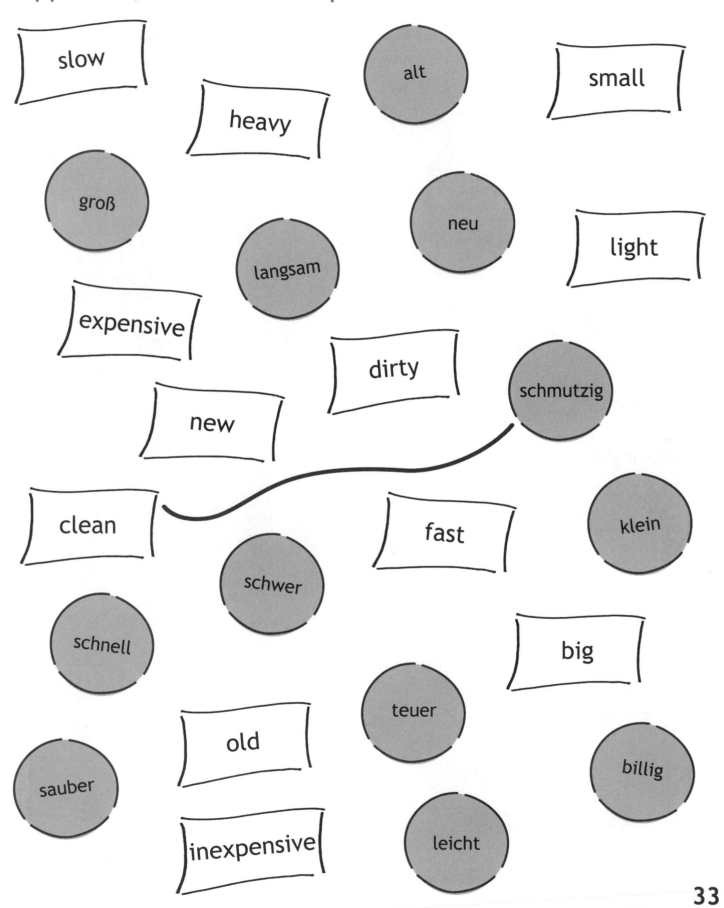

Finally, join the English words to their German opposites, as in the example.

slow

heavy

alt

small

groß

neu

light

langsam

expensive

dirty

schmutzig

new

clean

fast

klein

schwer

schnell

big

old

teuer

sauber

billig

inexpensive

leicht

33

❻ ANIMALS

Look at the pictures.
Tear out the flashcards for this topic.
Follow steps 1 and 2 of the plan in the introduction.

die Ente *dee entuh*

der Esel
dair aizel

die Katze
dee katsuh

der Hund
dair hunnd

das Kaninchen
das kaneenghen

der Affe
dair affuh

der Fisch *dair fish*

das Schaf *das shahf*

die Maus *dee mowss*

die Kuh *dee koo*

das Pferd
das pfaird

der Stier
dair shteer

◎ **M**atch the animals to their associated pictures, as in the example.

das Kaninchen

der Affe

das Pferd

die Katze

das Schaf

die Maus

der Hund

die Kuh

der Fisch

○ **S**omeone has ripped up the German words for animals. Can you join the two halves of the words, as the example?

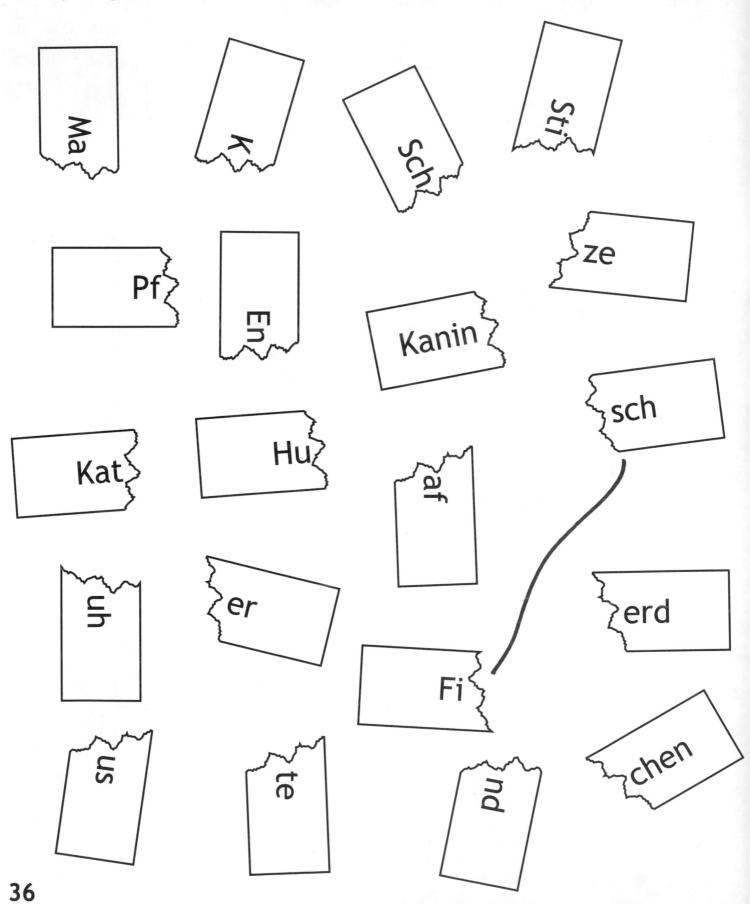

Ma

K

Sch

Sti

Pf

En

ze

Kanin

sch

Kat

Hu

af

uh

er

erd

Fi

us

te

nd

chen

36

Check (✔) the animal words you can find in the word pile.

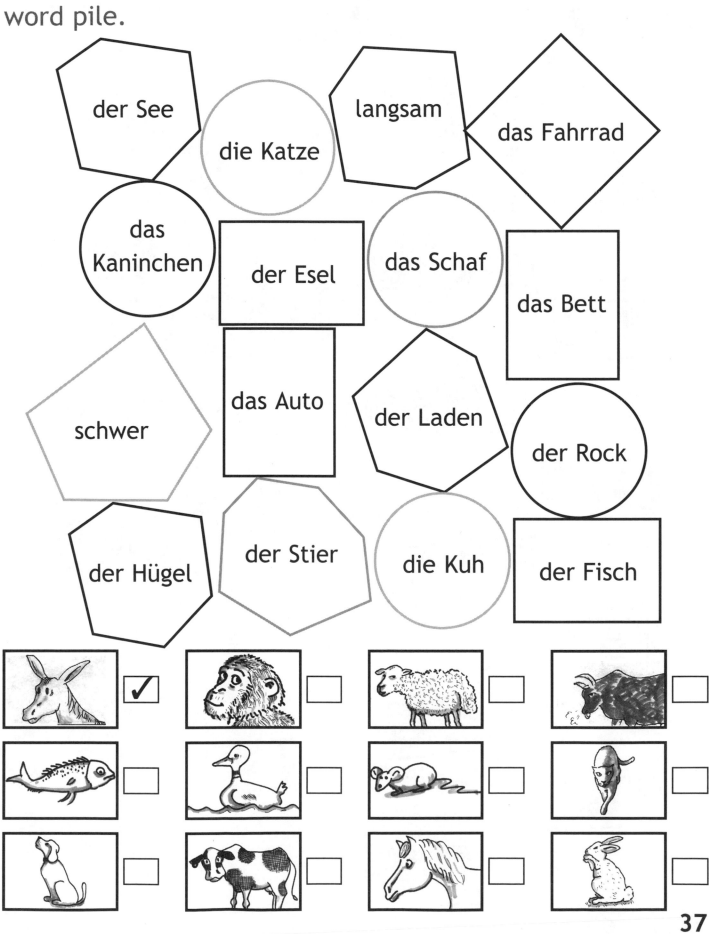

der See

die Katze

langsam

das Fahrrad

das Kaninchen

der Esel

das Schaf

das Bett

schwer

das Auto

der Laden

der Rock

der Hügel

der Stier

die Kuh

der Fisch

Join the German animals to their English equivalents.

monkey

der Hund

cow

der Stier

der Affe

mouse

dog

der Esel

sheep

das Kaninchen

fish ——————— der Fisch

bull

die Maus

donkey

die Ente

cat

die Kuh

duck

das Schaf

rabbit

das Pferd

horse

die Katze

38

⑦ PARTS OF THE BODY

Look at the pictures of parts of the body.
Tear out the flashcards for this topic.
Follow steps 1 and 2 of the plan in the introduction.

der Finger
dair finger

der Kopf
dair kopf

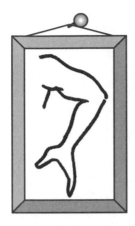

das Auge *das owguh*

der Arm
dair arm

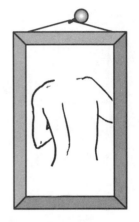

der Rücken
dair rewken

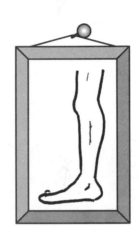

das Bein
das bine

die Hand
dee hannd

die Haare *dee hahruh*

der Bauch
dair bowkh

das Ohr
das ohr

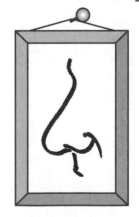

die Nase
dee nahzuh

der Mund
dair munnd

39

Match the pictures with the words, as in the example.

der Kopf

der Bauch

der Arm

das Auge

die Hand

die Haare

der Finger

der Rücken

- -

See if you can find and circle six parts of the body in the word square, then draw them in the boxes below.

The words can run left to right, or top to bottom:

S	C	H	A	A	R	E	T
I	C	U	M	H	R	B	I
C	M	L	U	S	V	O	V
B	E	I	N	H	R	U	A
R	I	A	D	A	L	C	N
I	N	N	N	A	S	E	E
O	R	E	I	D	L	E	E
O	H	R	P	R	T	A	T

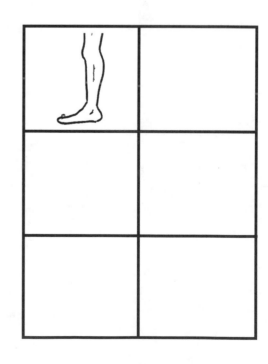

40

Write the words in the correct column, as in the example.

der	die	das
der Kopf		

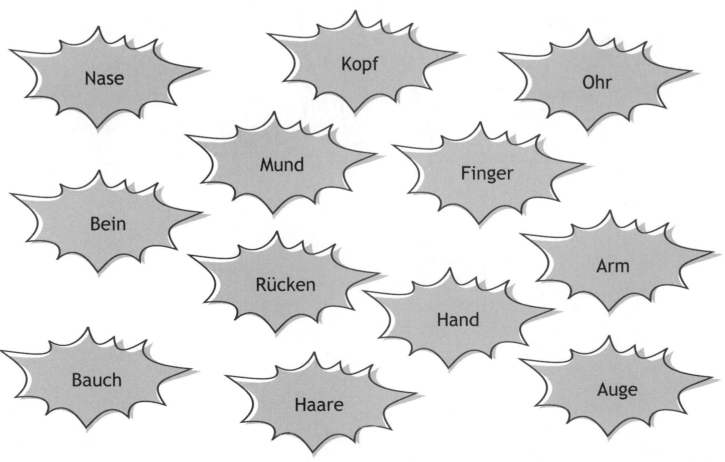

Label the body with the correct number, and write **der**, **die**, or **das** in front of the words.

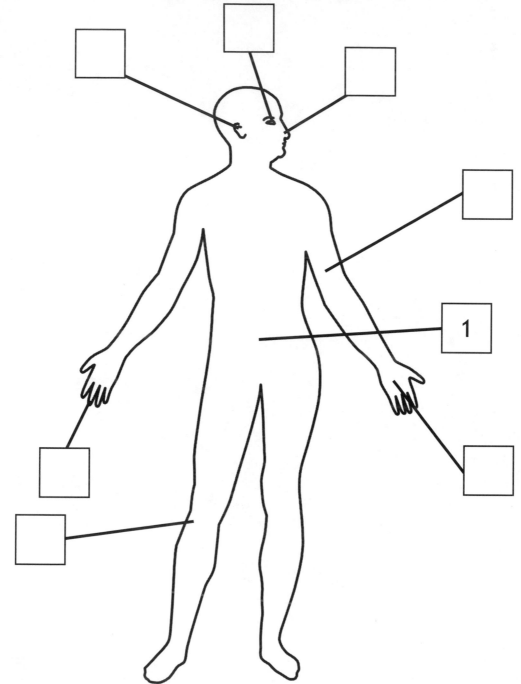

1 ___ Bauch   2 ___ Arm

3 ___ Nase   4 ___ Hand

5 ___ Ohr   6 ___ Bein

7 ___ Auge   8 ___ Finger

Finally, match the German words, their pronunciation, and the English meanings, as in the example.

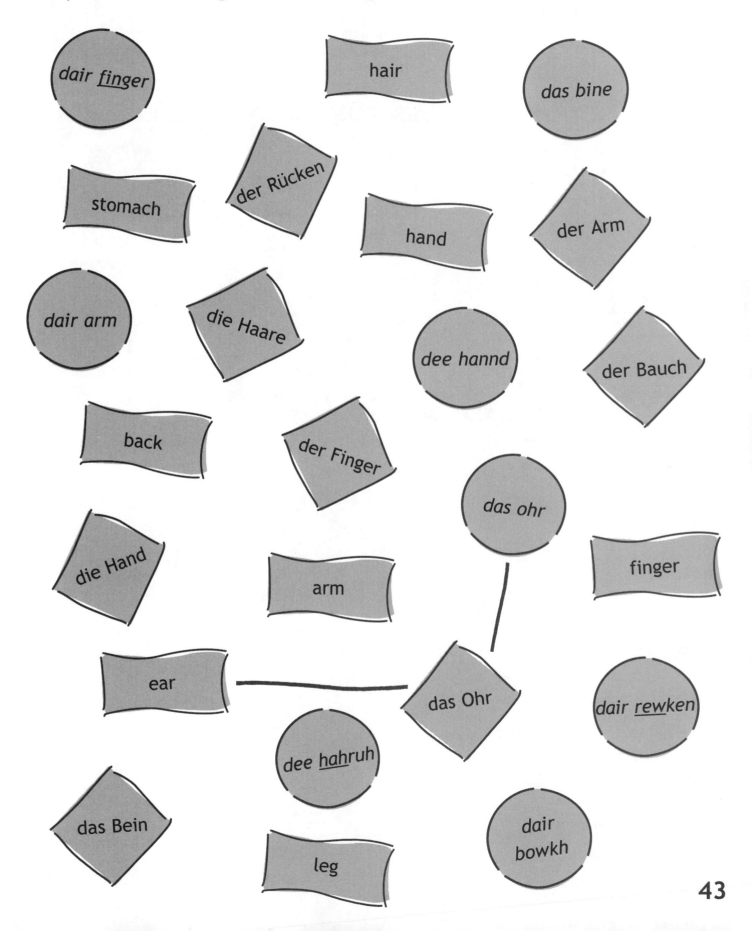

dair _finger_

hair

das bine

der Rücken

stomach

hand

der Arm

dair arm

die Haare

dee hannd

der Bauch

back

der Finger

das ohr

die Hand

arm

finger

ear

das Ohr

dair _rewken_

dee _hahruh_

das Bein

leg

dair bowkh

⑧ USEFUL EXPRESSIONS

Look at the pictures.
Tear out the flashcards for this topic.
Follow steps 1 and 2 of the plan in the introduction.

wo? *vo*

guten Tag
gooten tahg

auf Wiedersehen
owf veeder-zay-en

nein
nine

ja
yah

gestern
gestern

heute
hoytuh

morgen
morgen

hier *heer*

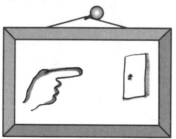

dort *dort*

jetzt
yetst

wie viel?
vee feel

Entschuldigung
entshuldigung

toll! *toll*

bitte *bittuh*

danke *dankuh*

Match the German words to their English equivalents.

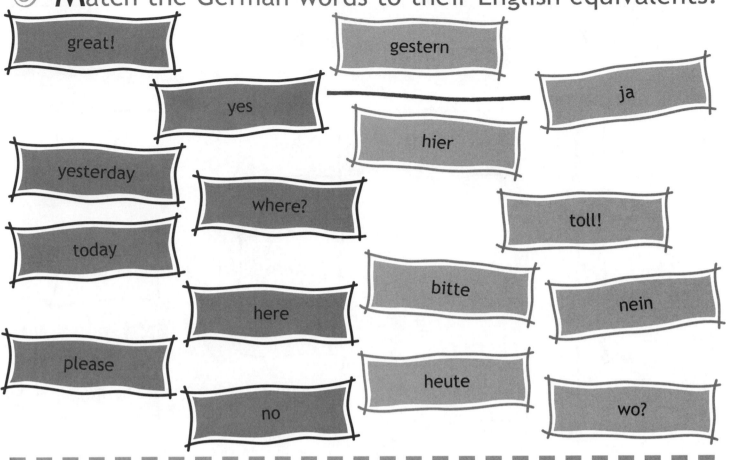

great!

gestern

yes

ja

hier

yesterday

where?

toll!

today

bitte

here

nein

please

heute

wo?

no

Fill in the missing letters in these expressions.

g _ s t _ r _

E _ _ s c _ u _ d _ _ _ n g

_ e u _ e

_ e _ z _

d _ n _ _

w _ e _ i _ l?

_ e _ n

t _ l _ !

m o _ _ e _

d _ _ t

Choose the German word that matches the picture to fill in the English word at the bottom of the page.

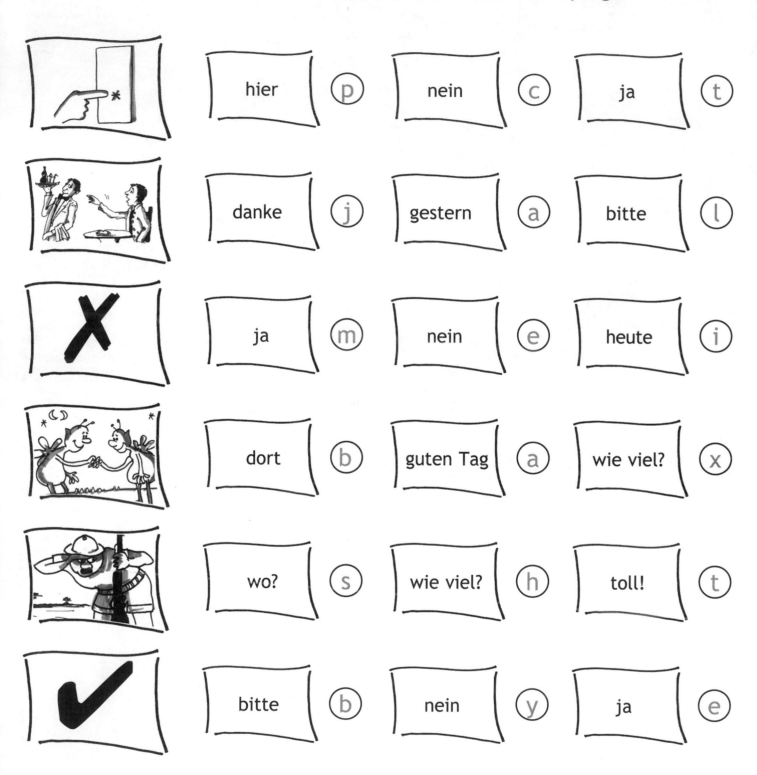

Picture			
door	hier (p)	nein (c)	ja (t)
waiter	danke (j)	gestern (a)	bitte (l)
X	ja (m)	nein (e)	heute (i)
ants	dort (b)	guten Tag (a)	wie viel? (x)
hunter	wo? (s)	wie viel? (h)	toll! (t)
check	bitte (b)	nein (y)	ja (e)

English word: (p) ( ) ( ) ( ) ( ) ( )

What are these people saying? Write the correct number in each speech bubble, as in the example.

1 guten Tag   2 bitte   3 ja   4 nein

5 hier   6 Entschuldigung 7 wo?   8 wie viel?

⊚ **F**inally, match the German words, their pronunciation, and the English meanings, as in the example.

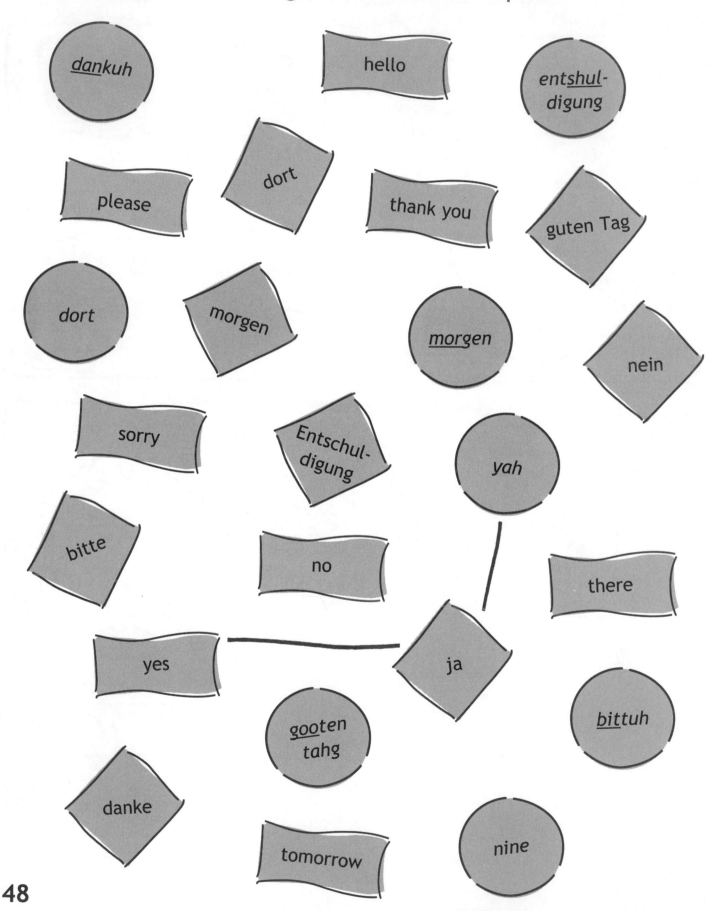

dankuh

hello

entshul-digung

dort

please

thank you

guten Tag

dort

morgen

morgen

nein

sorry

Entschul-digung

yah

bitte

no

there

yes

ja

bittuh

gooten tahg

danke

tomorrow

nine

● ROUND-UP

This section is designed to review all the 100 words you have met in the different topics. It is a good idea to test yourself with your flashcards before trying this section.

◎ The ten objects below are all in the picture. Can you find and circle them?

die Tür   die Blume   das Bett   der Mantel   der Hut

das Fahrrad   der Stuhl   der Hund   der Fisch   die Socke

© **S**ee if you can remember all these words.

heute

der Bäcker

schnell

die Nase

der Regen

ja

der Schrank

der Stier

das Kleid

billig

der Fluss

das Bein

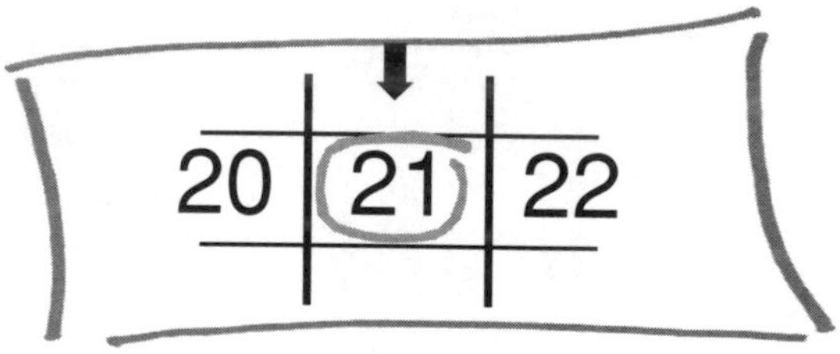

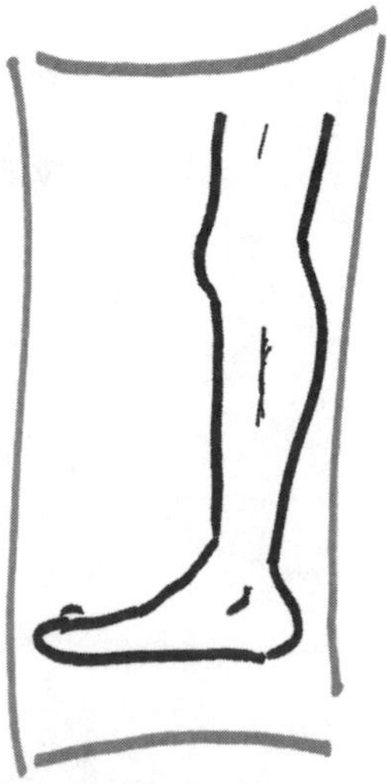

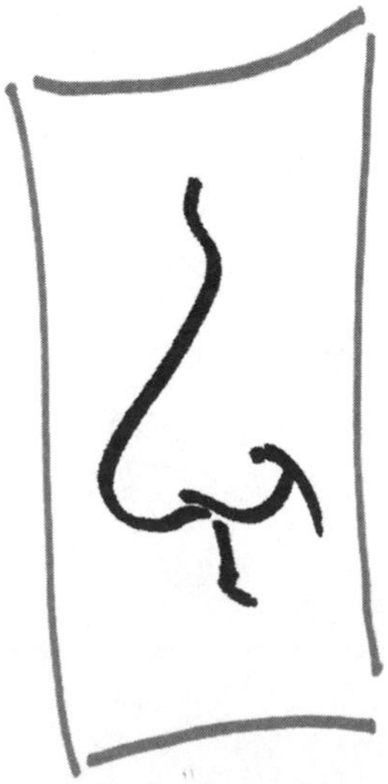

◎ **F**ind the odd one out in these groups of words and say why.

der Hund	die Kuh	(der Tisch)	der Affe

Because it isn't an animal.

- - - - - - - - -

der Bauernhof	der Mantel	das Hemd	der Rock

- - - - - - - -

das Meer	der See	der Fluss	das Feld

- - - - - - - -

teuer	groß	sauber	der Lastwagen

- - - - - - - -

das Kaninchen	die Katze	der Fisch	der Stier

- - - - - - - -

der Arm	das Sofa	der Kopf	der Bauch

- - - - - - - - -

guten Tag	gestern	morgen	heute

- - - - - - -

der Herd	das Bett	der Schrank	der Kühl-schrank

◎ **L**ook at the objects below for 30 seconds.

◎ **C**over the picture and try to remember all the objects. Circle the German words for those objects you remember.

die Blume

der Schuh

danke

die Tür

das Auto

nein

hier

der Mantel

der Lastwagen

der Gürtel

der Berg

der Stuhl

das Pferd

der Hut

die Socke

der Schlips

das Auge

das Bett

der Schal

die Bank

der Teppich

der Affe

Now match the German words, their pronunciation, and the English meanings, as in the example.

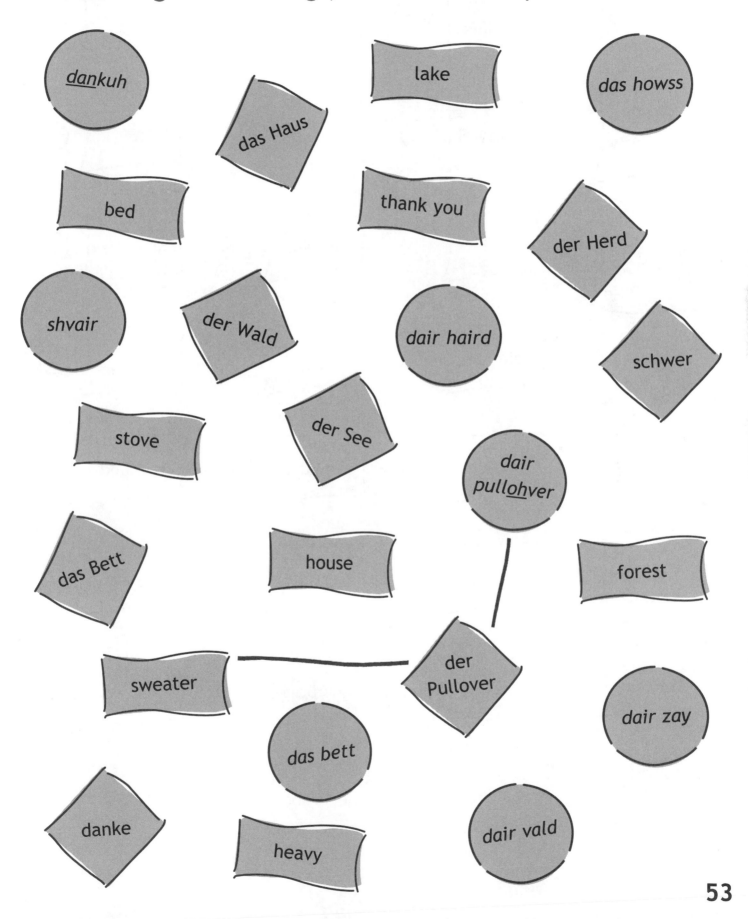

dankuh

lake

das howss

das Haus

bed

thank you

der Herd

shvair

der Wald

dair haird

schwer

stove

der See

dair pullohver

das Bett

house

forest

sweater

der Pullover

dair zay

das bett

danke

dair vald

heavy

Fill in the English phrase at the bottom of the page.

das Sofa (w)	die Bank (g)	das Ohr (t)
der Mantel (o)	der See (a)	die Brücke (e)
wo? (m)	wie viel? (l)	morgen (i)
die Kuh (b)	das Fenster (l)	der Metzger (h)
das Haus (e)	der Mund (a)	der Hund (d)
das Auge (o)	das Ohr (p)	die Maus (v)
der Hügel (n)	die Brücke (y)	das Kleid (r)
der Affe (n)	die Straße (e)	die Fabrik (s)

English phrase:

Look at the two pictures and check (✔) the objects that are different in Picture B.

Picture A

Picture B

der Rock	
die Hose	
die Tür	
die Katze	
der Stuhl	
der Fisch	
die Socke	
der Hund	

Now join the German words to their English equivalents.

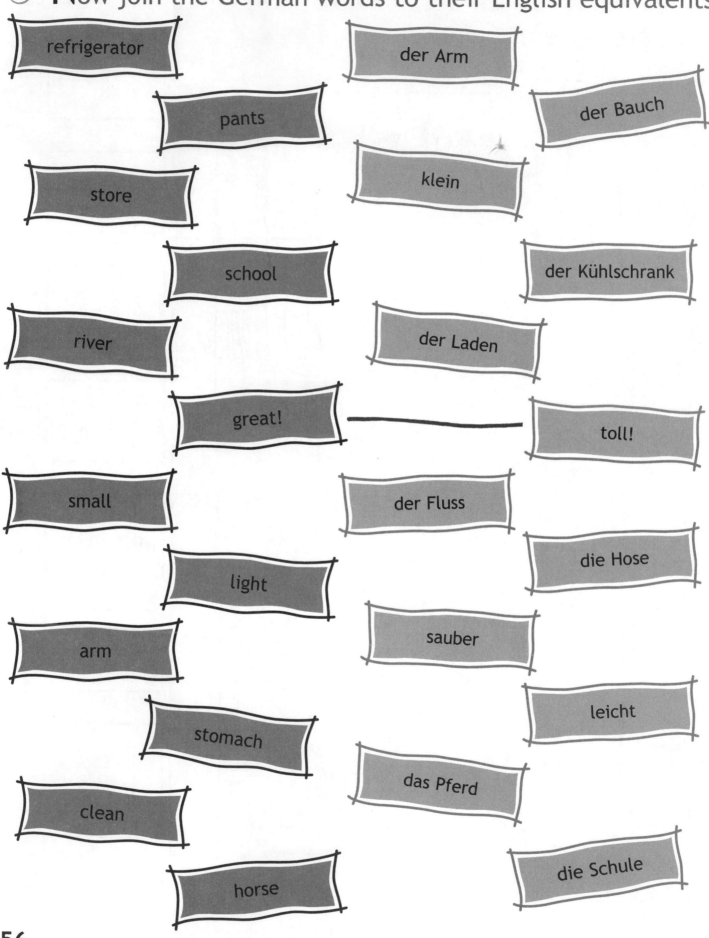

refrigerator

der Arm

pants

der Bauch

store

klein

school

der Kühlschrank

river

der Laden

great! ———————— toll!

small

der Fluss

light

die Hose

arm

sauber

stomach

leicht

clean

das Pferd

horse

die Schule

Complete the crossword using the picture clues.

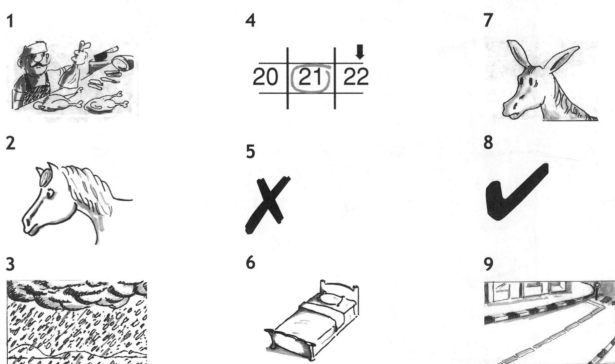

◎ Snake game.

- You will need a die and counter(s). You can challenge yourself to reach the finish or play with someone else. You have to throw the exact number to finish.

- Throw the die and move forward that number of spaces. When you land on a word you must pronounce it (with **der**, **die**, or **das** if appropriate) and say what it means in English. If you can't, you have to go back to the square you came from.

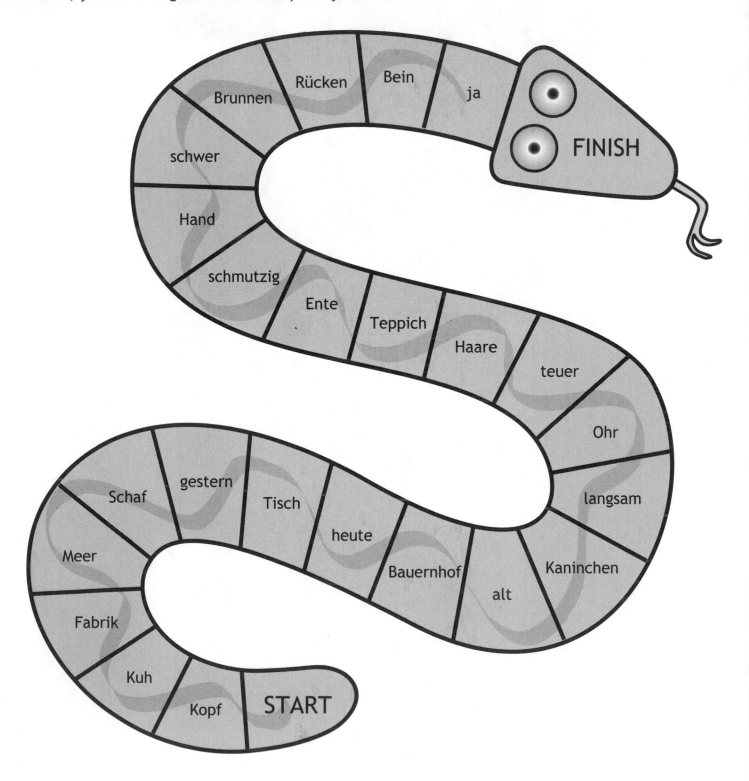

⊙ Answers

❶ AROUND THE HOME

Page 10 (top)
See page 9 for correct picture.

Page 10 (bottom)

door	die Tür
cupboard	der Schrank
stove	der Herd
bed	das Bett
table	der Tisch
chair	der Stuhl
refrigerator	der Kühlschrank
computer	der Computer

Page 11 (top)

Stuhl	Schrank
Bord	Fenster
Teppich	Tür
Kühlschrank	Bett
Herd	Tisch

Page 11 (bottom)

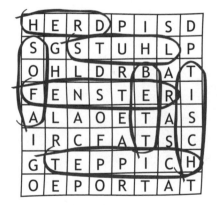

Page 12

Page 13
English word: window

❷ CLOTHES

Page 15 (top)

die Hose	der Rock
der Schal	der Gürtel
das Kleid	der Schlips
der Mantel	der Hut

Page 15 (bottom)

Page 16

hat	der Hut	*dair hoot*
shoe	der Schuh	*dair shoo*
sock	die Socke	*dee zokuh*
scarf	der Schal	*dair shahl*
tie	der Schlips	*dair shlips*
belt	der Gürtel	*dair gewrtel*
coat	der Mantel	*dair manntel*
pants	die Hose	*dee hohzuh*

Page 17

Hut (hat)	1
Mantel (coat)	0
Gürtel (belt)	2
Schuh (shoe)	2 (1 pair)
Hose (pants)	1
Schal (scarf)	1
Kleid (dress)	0
Socke (sock)	6 (3 pairs)
Rock (skirt)	0
Schlips (tie)	2
Hemd (shirt)	4
Pullover (sweater)	1

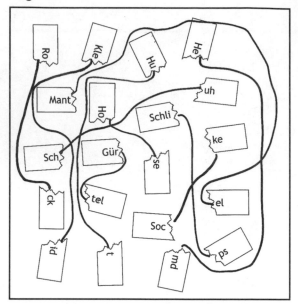

❸ AROUND TOWN

Page 20 (top)

truck	der Lastwagen
store	der Laden
factory	die Fabrik
bench	die Bank
car	das Auto
fountain	der Brunnen
school	die Schule
house	das Haus

Page 20 (bottom)

bicycle	4
bench	7
house	2
fountain	6
truck	1
road	3
car	5

Page 21

1 die Bank

2 das Auto

3 der Brunnen

4 die Fabrik

5 der Lastwagen

6 die Schule

7 die Straße

8 der Metzger

9 der Bäcker

Page 22

English word: school

Page 23

der	die	das
der Laden	die Fabrik	das Haus
der Bäcker	die Bank	das Auto
der Lastwagen	die Schule	das Fahrrad
der Brunnen	die Straße	
der Metzger		

❹ COUNTRYSIDE

Page 25

See page 24 for correct picture.

Page 26

Brücke	✔	Feld	✔
Baum	✔	Wald	✔
Regen	✗	See	✗
Hügel	✗	Fluss	✔
Berg	✔	Blume	✔
Meer	✗	Bauernhof	✗

Page 27 (top)

der Regen	die Brücke
der Fluss	der Bauernhof
der Baum	der See
das Meer	der Hügel

Page 27 (bottom)

T	E	P	C	D	A	P	E
I	C	C	F	L	U	S	S
F	L	R	E	G	E	N	F
C	B	B	L	E	R	T	L
W	A	L	D	M	E	R	B
A	U	U	N	I	S	E	E
U	M	M	T	A	G	N	R
P	E	E	A	E	N	N	G

sea	das Meer	*das mair*
lake	der See	*dair zay*
rain	der Regen	*dair raigen*
farm	der Bauernhof	*dair bowern-hohf*
flower	die Blume	*dee bloomuh*
mountain	der Berg	*dair bairg*
river	der Fluss	*dair fluss*
field	das Feld	*das feld*

➎ OPPOSITES

Page 30

expensive	teuer
big	groß
light	leicht
slow	langsam
clean	sauber
inexpensive	billig
dirty	schmutzig
small	klein
heavy	schwer
new	neu
fast	schnell
old	alt

Page 31

English word: change

Page 32

Odd one outs are those which are not opposites:

schwer
klein
neu
schmutzig
langsam
billig

Page 33

old	neu
big	klein
new	alt
slow	schnell
dirty	sauber

small	groß
heavy	leicht
clean	schmutzig
light	schwer
expensive	billig
inexpensive	teuer
fast	langsam

➏ ANIMALS

Page 35

die Kuh   das Kaninchen   der Fisch

das Schaf   der Hund   der Affe

das Pferd   die Maus   die Katze

Page 36

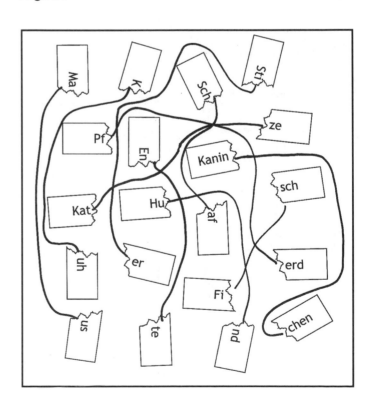

61

Page 37

donkey	✔	mouse	✘
monkey	✘	cat	✔
sheep	✔	dog	✘
bull	✔	cow	✔
fish	✔	horse	✘
duck	✘	rabbit	✔

Page 38

monkey	der Affe
cow	die Kuh
mouse	die Maus
dog	das Hund
sheep	das Schaf
fish	der Fisch
bull	der Stier
donkey	der Esel
cat	die Katze
duck	die Ente
rabbit	das Kaninchen
horse	das Pferd

❼ PARTS OF THE BODY

Page 40 (top)

See page 39 for correct picture.

Page 40 (bottom)

S	C	H	A	A	R	E	T
I	C	U	M	H	R	B	I
C	M	L	U	S	V	O	V
B	E	I	N	H	R	U	A
R	I	A	D	A	L	C	N
I	N	N	N	N	A	S	E
O	R	E	I	D	L	E	E
O	H	R	P	R	T	A	T

You should have also drawn pictures of:
leg; mouth; ear; nose; hand; hair

Page 41

der	die	das
der Kopf	*die Hand*	*das Auge*
der Arm	*die Haare*	*das Bein*
der Finger	*die Nase*	*das Ohr*
der Bauch		
der Rücken		
der Mund		

Page 42

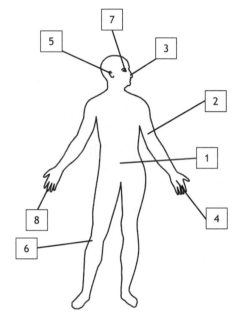

1	der Bauch	2	der Arm
3	die Nase	4	die Hand
5	das Ohr	6	das Bein
7	das Auge	8	der Finger

Page 43

ear	das Ohr	*das ohr*
hair	die Haare	*dee <u>hahr</u>uh*
hand	die Hand	*dee hannd*
stomach	der Bauch	*dair bowkh*
arm	der Arm	*dair arm*
back	der Rücken	*dair <u>rewken</u>*
finger	der Finger	*dair <u>finger</u>*
leg	das Bein	*das bine*

8 USEFUL EXPRESSIONS

Page 45 (top)

great!	toll!
yes	ja
yesterday	gestern
where?	wo?
today	heute
here	hier
please	bitte
no	nein

Page 45 (bottom)

gestern	Entschuldigung
heute	jetzt
danke	wie viel?
nein	toll!
morgen	dort

Page 46

English word: please

Page 47

Page 48

yes	ja	*yah*
hello	guten Tag	*gooten tahg*
no	nein	*nine*
sorry	Entschuldigung	*entshuldigung*
please	bitte	*bittuh*
there	dort	*dort*
thank you	danke	*dankuh*
tomorrow	morgen	*morgen*

● ROUND-UP

Page 49

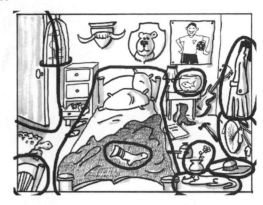

Page 50

= der Regen
= der Stier
= ja
= der Schrank
= billig
= heute
= der Fluss
= die Nase
= das Kleid
= das Bein
= schnell
= der Bäcker

Page 51

der Tisch (Because it isn't an animal.)

der Bauernhof (Because it isn't an item of clothing.)

das Feld (Because it isn't connected with water.)

der Lastwagen (Because it isn't a descriptive word.)

der Fisch (Because it lives in water/doesn't have legs.)

das Sofa (Because it isn't a part of the body.)

guten Tag (Because it isn't an expression of time.)

das Bett (Because you wouldn't find it in the kitchen.)

Page 52

Words that appear in the picture:

der Schlips

das Auto

die Blume

der Schuh

der Hut

der Lastwagen

der Affe

der Teppich

der Stuhl

der Gürtel

der Schal

Page 53

sweater	der Pullover	*dair pullohver*
lake	der See	*dair zay*
thank you	danke	*dankuh*
bed	das Bett	*das bett*
house	das Haus	*das howss*
forest	der Wald	*dair vald*
stove	der Herd	*dair haird*
heavy	schwer	*shvair*

Page 54

English phrase: well done!

Page 55

der Rock	✗
die Hose	✔ (shade)
die Tür	✔ (handle)
die Katze	✗
der Stuhl	✔ (back)
der Fisch	✔ (direction)
die Socke	✔ (pattern)
der Hund	✗

Page 56

refrigerator	der Kühlschrank
pants	die Hose
store	der Laden
school	die Schule
river	der Fluss
great!	toll!
small	klein
light	leicht
arm	der Arm
stomach	der Bauch
clean	sauber
horse	das Pferd

Page 57

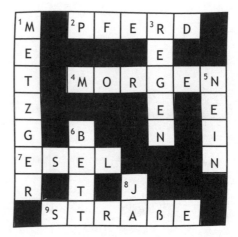

Page 58

Here are the English equivalents of the word, in order from START to FINISH:

head	der Kopf	ear	das Ohr
cow	die Kuh	expensive	teuer
factory	die Fabrik	hair	die Haare
sea	das Meer	rug	der Teppich
sheep	das Schaf	duck	die Ente
yesterday	gestern	dirty	schmutzig
table	der Tisch	hand	die Hand
today	heute	heavy	schwer
farm	der Bauernhof	fountain	der Brunnen
old	alt	back	der Rücken
rabbit	das Kaninchen	leg	das Bein
slow	langsam	yes	ja

der Computer

das Fenster

der Tisch

der Schrank

der Kühlschrank

der Stuhl

das Sofa

der Herd

die Tür

das Bett

das Bord

der Teppich

window	computer
cupboard	table
chair	refrigerator
stove	sofa
bed	door
rug	shelf

der Gürtel	der Mantel
der Rock	der Hut
der Schlips	der Schuh
der Pullover	das Hemd
der Schal	die Socke
die Hose	das Kleid

coat	belt
hat	skirt
shoe	tie
shirt	sweater
sock	scarf
dress	pants

die Schule	das Auto
die Straße	der Lastwagen
die Fabrik	der Laden
die Bank	das Fahrrad
der Metzger	der Bäcker
der Brunnen	das Haus

car	school
truck	road
store	factory
bicycle	bench
baker	butcher
house	fountain

der See

der Wald

der Hügel

das Meer

der Berg

der Baum

der Regen

die Blume

die Brücke

der Fluss

der Bauernhof

das Feld

forest	lake
sea	hill
tree	mountain
flower	rain
river	bridge
field	farm

schwer	leicht
groß	klein
alt	neu
schnell	langsam
sauber	schmutzig
billig	teuer

light	heavy
small	big
new	old
slow	fast
dirty	clean
expensive	inexpensive

die Ente

die Katze

die Maus

die Kuh

das Kaninchen

der Hund

das Pferd

der Affe

der Stier

der Fisch

der Esel

das Schaf

cat	duck
cow	mouse
dog	rabbit
monkey	horse
fish	bull
sheep	donkey

der Arm

der Finger

der Kopf

der Mund

das Ohr

das Bein

die Hand

der Bauch

das Auge

die Haare

die Nase

der Rücken

finger	arm
mouth	head
leg	ear
stomach	hand
hair	eye
back	nose

bitte	danke
ja	nein
guten Tag	auf Wiedersehen
gestern	heute
morgen	wo?
hier	dort
Entschuldigung	wie viel?
toll!	jetzt

thank you	please
no	yes
goodbye	hello
today	yesterday
where?	tomorrow
there	here
how much?	sorry!
now	great!